D0461662

Elegy Owed

ALSO BY BOB HICOK

Words for Empty and Words for Full

This Clumsy Living

Insomnia Diary

Animal Soul

Plus Shipping

The Legend of Light

Hicok, Bob, 1960–
Elegy owed /

c2013.
33305227962671
mi   05/15/13

BOB HICOK

Elegy Owed

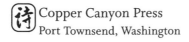

Copper Canyon Press
Port Townsend, Washington

Copyright 2013 by Bob Hicok

All rights reserved

Printed in the United States of America

Cover art: *Bloodroot*. Archival Epson print on Dibond with mixed media and varnish. Robert & Shana ParkeHarrison. 2008

Copper Canyon Press is in residence at Fort Worden State Park in Port Townsend, Washington, under the auspices of Centrum. Centrum is a gathering place for artists and creative thinkers from around the world, students of all ages and backgrounds, and audiences seeking extraordinary cultural enrichment.

LIBRARY OF CONGRESS CATALOGING-IN-PUBLICATION DATA

Hicok, Bob, 1960–
Elegy owed / Bob Hicok.
    pages   cm
ISBN 978-1-55659-436-6 (hardcover : alk. paper)
1. Title.
PS3558.I28E44 2013
811'.54 — dc23

2012043531

9 8 7 6 5 4 3 2 FIRST PRINTING

COPPER CANYON PRESS
Post Office Box 271
Port Townsend, Washington 98368

www.coppercanyonpress.org

for Eve

ACKNOWLEDGMENTS

I would like to thank the editors and staff of the following magazines and websites for publishing some of the poems that appear in this book:

The American Poetry Review, The Believer, Blackbird, Blip Magazine, Conduit, diode, Fifth Wednesday Journal, The Good Men Project, Green Mountains Review, The Iowa Review, The Kenyon Review, Lo-Ball, Narrative, New England Review, Octopus Magazine, The Offending Adam, The Paris Review, Poemeleon, Scythe, The Southern Review, Swink, and *Vinyl Poetry.*

"As I was saying," "Confessions of a nature lover," and "Equine aubade" were published in *The New Yorker.*

"Leave a message" was published in *The New York Times.*

Some of the poems in this book appeared in the chapbooks *Speaking American* (YesYes Books, 2013), and *Exuberance* (Floating Wolf Quarterly, 2012).

Contents

Elegy Owed

Pilgrimage

My heart is cold,
it should wear a mitten. My heart
is whatever temperature a heart is
in a man who doesn't believe in heaven.

I found half
an old Barbie in a field
and bathed her torso
in a coffee can of rain, put a deer skull
with antlers in a window
to watch with empty sockets
deer go by, these are souls
given the best care
I can manage, a pigeon died
and I gave it to the river.
If lightning
loved me, it would be sewn
with tongues, it would open
my mind to the sky
within the sky.

I put birds
in most poems and rivers, put rivers
in most birds and thinking, put the dead
in many sentences
blinking quietly, put missing
into bed with having, put wolves
in my mouth hunting whispers, put faith
in making, each poem a breath
nailed to nothing.

Elegy with lies

This lost person I loved. Loved for a hundred years.
When I find her. Find her in a forest. In a cabin
under smoke and clouds shaped like smoke. When I find her
and call her name (nothing) and knock (nothing)
and build a machine that believes it's God and the machine
calls her name (nothing) and knocks (nothing).
When I tear the machine down and she runs from the cabin
pointing a gun at my memories and telling me
to leave, stranger, leave, man of hammers.
When I can't finish that story. When I get to the gun
pointed at my head. When I want it to go off.
When everything I say to anyone all day long
is bang. That would be today. When I can't use her name.
All day long. Soft as cotton, tender as kiss. Bang.

The days are getting longer

The birds I feed seed every morning
never thank me, I tell on them
to my mother, who I assume
raised them and everything
from pups. She's begun to forget
why my voice shows up in her ear
each week, let alone
what the real name of the ruby-
throated-whatsit is, it's hard
to help the dead be dead
before they are. Mourning

doves, cardinals, chickadees
strip the cupboard bare
in a matter of hours,
as tiny guillotines cut each leaf
from every tree, the leaves
fall orange & brown, a muted rainbow
arting-up the forgiveness
of October air, which smells naked,
new, and accepts the shape
of everything in its mouth. She asked

the other day how my day was,
I told her, she asked again,
as if I hadn't answered
or slept in the rumpus-room
of her womb. Do you ever look
at a crust of bread and wonder
if that's God, if the quiet

that lives there is the same hush
we become? I never do too,
but is it, and why are we dragging
these anvils behind us?

O

I'm thinking I watched a man and his son holding hands as they
      crossed a parking lot

last night, thinking I was moved by the root or lifeboat or ladder of the
      father's arm

into the life of the son, the root or labyrinth of his arm as they moved
      at the pace

of the child, whose walking still bore signs of the womb, of being
      wobbly water and I wanted

to reverse my vasectomy on the spot and have a child with the moon,
      I wish there were a word

that was the thing it was the word of, that when I said *sun* I could be
      sun, all of it in my mouth,

burning, you might think and be so marvelously right about praise that
      you open your door

one day and the day walks in and stays for years

The story of 5:33

The sense of someone turning in what wasn't exactly
a dream or wakefulness. She would be leaving soon and I
couldn't sleep and wouldn't get up. Like someone was there
or to say, someone was there, puts them there, which is
a place in the sense that any name derived from a place
or region is a place, as in, these thoughts are their own
pants or favorite drinks, if we are talking about people.
She would be leaving soon for her mother's for a week,
someone turning on the other side of a door after saying
something like, *we should slap the shit out of morning*
so it leaves us alone in bed. It could be argued
that any change from a steady state is violent, as now,
I hear a cat in what had been an absence of cat,
a breaking of a truce between the levels
of crow-chatter and the background hissing of the universe,
if we are talking about people. The sense of someone
turning to look back in the most casual way
someone might look back, not to ask the day to follow,
or with anchored gaze, or to distend the shape of time,
though as an object, I am full
of these brushings of drums, these paintings
hung on air until the walls arrive. Almost as if I am
a voyeur of my thoughts, in the sense that boats don't ask
permission of water to float or drown, though water
reflects these choices while going about its business.
Had I time, and pins, and thread, I would poke myself
all over and connect the sovereign drops of blood
in a map for a lost child who realizes she had wanted
since she was born to run away. The sense of someone turning
toward the magnetism of wild flowers, if we are talking

about people. Then I was here, looking back through an opening
that is vined or bricked or flesh-hewn, the dress of it
changing as someone turned toward their sense
of someone turning, a wave the gesture that comes to mind
now, if it's not too late to rub the day and make a wish.

Knockturn

Tiptoeing through the grass
not to wake the grass, sheet music
for the laments all over the field
like wings of moonlight, crickets
hushing their banter around my ankles,
then remembering they're an ocean
once I've passed, I enjoy thinking of solitude
when I'm alone as the spouse of living
with others, who are often sharp
in my experience and pointy, people
are like scissors, you shouldn't run with them,
I should go back and tell my wife
my skin is a photograph, a slow exposure
of stars she can touch
with the swirls, the galaxies
of her fingerprints when she wakes
and gives me the dream report,
decades she's been late for a test
or taken it naked, I would go
to that school, I would major
in Yes, the dark is my favorite suit to wear
where bear are also
sometimes, and coyote, and the dead
get to be whatever they want as far
as I can tell, the less I can see,
the more personally I take the little
I can make out with,
holding what I am held by, the night
and I almost the same smudge
of whatever this is, it is seductive

to wade into and slip away and not drown,
my life the only thing that has been with me
my whole life

Good-bye, topspin

Life has taken my cartilage and left me a biography of André Breton.

I will limp persuasively and write you a letter sprinkled with
      French surrealism.

This doesn't feel like but is truly my good-bye to youth as I practiced it
      when I was young.

What a lovely time you showed me, cartilage, heart, elbows, pineal gland.

There was a party and I was invited.

There was sprinting and wind looked at me like a brother.

There was yee-hah and it was me injecting complacency with
      that hoedown.

But nostalgia:
go to hell.

Not going to do that.

Not going to be a lamprey on the side of the past, sucking for dear life,
      since I have had
and am having a dear life.

Thank you sweat glands, shin splints, kidney stones, proprioception
for telling me where I am in space in relation to sunlight, breasts, saffron,
life.

Here.

Here is where I am in space.

Here is where space is in me.

Elegy to hunger

There's a strain of cannibalism
I admire. A beloved has died. A hole
has been dug to be filled or a boat dragged
across a mile of silence to burn
upon the forgetfulness of water. One person
or twenty stand at the hole or the boat
& the body stares through closed eyes. The body
turning gray, filling with clouds, with a rain
that will last until flood. One person
takes a bite and means it, not a nibble
but a devotion, we are locusts
after all. Then the others,
until the body is clothed
with unspeaking ghosts
of mouths, the body an absence
bearing absences. The bite. The soul.
The swallow. Eating the hours
she filled, the shadow she cast. And I.
I should have.

Coming to life

He was made to touch a corpse as a child. His aunt's. Mother's side.
When he was very young, he'd hear that phrase — she's from your moth-
er's side — and imagine his aunt's head growing from his mother's ribs,
tiny like Barbie's. It was not exactly a vision, more of a thought he had,
usually late at night. He wondered if his mother had done his aunt's hair
like his sister did Barbie's, and asked her one morning, and she laughed,
and soon he was older. His mother was crying in the front row. The tan
folding chairs creaked when he sat down. A group of men, ties loose,
stood near a back door, stepping out now and then for cigarettes. Smoke
was alive in the sunlight, curling and twisting up like the woman he saw
dance on TV a few nights before, her dress nearly one long scarf. When
he put his head against his mother's shoulder, she slid it around to her
chest. He was almost too old for this, but no one said anything when he
rested his hand on her breast. They sat quite awhile. People came and
spoke of his aunt and Heaven and God. He closed his eyes and thought
the light he saw inside might be Heaven. It formed a circle and faded,
formed a circle and faded, as his mother hushed rosary beads through
her hands. He opened his eyes. They stood. His mother kissed his aunt
on each cheek and said something in her ear. *Where do the words go in a
dead person,* he decided to ask his mother later, but never did. When she
drew his hand toward his aunt's face, he didn't resist. He was like water
being lead to water. Drink this, feel. She felt like nothing, he would
tell a woman in college, their backs to the wall as they sat in bed. She'd
asked what he meant by nothing. It was just that, as if in the silence of
her skin, all possibilities had been taken away. But they had just made
love and he didn't want to bruise their warmth. *The opposite of this,* he
said, putting a finger to the mole on her knee. The rest of the afternoon,
it was as if someone had said to them, *Here are the brand-new bodies.
Open them.*

Ode to magic

Do the one where you bring the woman
back from the dead, his host, the king, commanded,
but the magician would not.

He did the one in which he was one half
of the folk-indie duo Heartwind.

He did the one that required a volunteer tornado
from the audience.

He did the one in which the lungs of a warlord
are filled with lava.

But he would not bring the woman back from the dead.

The king wanted to cut his head off
but the queen said, *Perhaps this is just a poem.*

This is just a poem.

Everyone is alive as long as the poem is alive.

The king wears a crown of a thousand crows.

The queen keeps three lovers inside the castle
of her dress, the third a spare for the second,
the second a technical advisor to the first.

The magician's tongue is nothing but the word
abracadabra and the dead woman has just written

cotton candy on her shopping list, just written
antelopes and reminded the poet
he is running out of things to say.

The queen asks him, *Do the one in which your heart*
is folded over and pounded with moonlight,
in which you claim to miss everything —
I like how big your arms are in that one,
your throat the size of the universe
before silence gets the last word.

Oh, that one, the poet says, *is this one,*
is the only one.

Listen to it sound like shucked corn,
like a single blade of grass eating sun,
like any train or noisemaker or hallelujah
that will keep this line from being
the last line, and this line
but not the coming line, the hush,
the crush it is.

Pre-planning

The gray pantry moths are back, the morning and I

already guilty of a double murder, then something black

flies and dies in my coffee, I drink anyway

while the insect's past sags and drips on the tip

of the tongue of a spoon, a light

above the sleeping table, the sun hours away

and I'm surrounded by death in poems, gaunt books stacked

unmortared along the walls, I'm home from pre-planning

digging my parents under, dark blue caskets, minimal flowers,

a few of the open questions: when

and who will carry them and was yesterday

the last I'll see them with capable eyes, what leaves

leaves the wonder of whatever resided, a mist, a powder,

certainly we are batteries, engines, storms, weather

our whole lives, soon my origins will resemble grass

when I go home and look down for them, who are brittle now

and not convincing when they speak of years

l ah g

Beside her death, forsythia. And everywhere
after: hills and storefronts, the dream
of the yellow pencil with which I wrote her name
to keep it lithe in the body of cursive. A sense
of calm, as a drowner who has said yes to water
might float a last bit unruffled by waves,
or like a metronome has grown in my eyes
and to look is to listen to the counting down
in all things: washing my hands, leaning
against a chain-link fence after two hours
of hitting serves, ball in a box, ball in a box,
a kind of sewing of myself into process,
into the distraction of chatter
by flesh, a love of form, suddenly,
how even the espoused shape of a rock
is a meditation. On what, exactly: the grammar
of the earth? What a palette for loss: forsythia,
redbud, some kind of apple I can never recall,
snow-capped trees on an eighty-degree day. I feel
I'm a mile above spring on a wire, trying to breathe
with an honor that doesn't offend balance,
that earns me in this second the next second
in which her life is my missing of her life.
Far below, yellow dot after yellow dot
leads me to the conclusion I like yellow
better now that it has come to me from so many
directions, from so deep a sleep
and touched me brightly/softly with its inadvertent
there there.

Sound scape

I recorded the woods and played this listening
back to the woods and wondered why we call it
playing catch and not playing throw.
The sound of goldenrod reminded me
that an empty shirtsleeve takes after a flute. Leaving a bar
twenty-eight years later, I realized
Betty Caulder was talking to me in handsprings
as a child I couldn't hear. Drunken stars
have been the kind of friends to nod and listen.
I never get this right: stars or planets
shimmer? Is shimmer the word for seeming always
about to break into song? Shimmering rocks,
shimmering dirt, the shimmering sense
that if I stopped wondering what follows this,
I'd feel a part, not apart. All I'd have asked,
my Incan heart removed from my chest,
is that the priest hold it to my ear
so I could hear myself inhabit the quiet.
Dear whisper: tell me a story
in which the hole is the hero. What falls
out, what reaches through.

You name this one

Trying to decide what's as beautiful
as a bucket of nails on a deck, rain by rust
almost blood-colored, almost life
starting over from nothing, I pick the moment
I didn't kill a milk snake, diverted
the spade at the last, harmlessly cutting
the ground, finally knowing the difference
between bright and poisonous. Or when

I realized *she loves me, she loves me not*
explains why daisies avoid us
as often as they can, I say *Run, simple flower,*
away from my need to know
anything at all, everything
would be better. Or when

I was given an electron microscope
by the Tooth Fairy, that was beautiful
too, to sleep painfully
on a deeper seeing, and wake, and cut
my mother's tongue to show her the cells
by which she told me, *Your toast*
is ready, sweetie. Which it was

every morning, buttered and jammed
and cut in half, an application
of disorder that created
a different sense of order. As when Chartres

is broken into a thousand
puzzle pieces and becomes
a system on a table
more interesting when a piece or two
or three go missing.

A request

The fact of an end, of gone having a moment, coordinates at which I stood
and have since lived stuck, looking then and now down at a bed,
      looking then
and now for an arm to move as an arm had moved, we say countless
though I could have counted the times, looking there when there has ceased
to be a place, looking when when when has ceased to be a point, is an
      always, a virus
of memory. And then she was aperture, pore, mouth, anus, vagina, was
      the opened Earth
and I was Orpheus, I am Orpheus, please the removal of my head to the
      river, the severing
of my singing tumbling all the way to the forgetting sea.

One of those things we say

My thoughts are with you.

They're the left sleeve of the white shirt in your closet,
at the far end, away from the other disguises of flesh.

The twist tie in your ponytail when all else fails.

I am here, weeks of walking away, Ohio and skin
between us, West Virginia and strip mines, I'd hate to count
the rivers, how many other women
with their dying mothers,
their long nights at the picnic table
with stars and the stars of cigarettes again
after so many years of no.

But my thoughts are there and my thoughts
are hands washing the oatmeal pot, taking out the diapers, breath
should come with a warning,

YOU WILL RAISE YOUR MOTHER INTO DEATH LIKE A CHILD

but you would, anyway, breathe.

Breathe and drop a red ball into a lake,
breathe and go to the prom,
breathe and throw a party for the house when the mortgage
has lost its teeth.

And there you are, old.
And as everyone else quits breathing, you keep on.

And then it's your turn to stop.
And in the second you do, you know something you can't tell us,
about after, about the story of here.
And your daughter, looking at your face, has no idea
you're trying to comfort her.

And you have no idea I'm trying to comfort you.

I love how intimate I've become with failure.

That leaves, having given up green for brown, sky for earth,
say things when I walk through them.

Gibberish, I think it's called.

Like my thoughts after six hundred miles of travel,
that shutter banging in wind, that dog
barking at nothing
because every time he's barked at nothing,
nothing's gone wrong and why not keep it that way?

Making do

Out here, no one would know

if I set the bit of human jaw I found under the house
on the grass above a dress, a flowered dress I stretch
to the full length of wind and walk away, giving memory
some privacy. A dress that appeared one morning
after a storm, beside the woman who'd been wearing it,
who asked if this was her life or some other window
being opened, and left before I could answer,
almost as if I'm making her and this poem and my past
up as I go, to help me feel nothing

goes to waste, not even waste.

The gift

My wife gave me a tie made of the thread
of life. I was afraid to wear a tie
made of the thread of life. That it would snag.
That I'd spill coffee on it. But I wore it,
and every person who looked at it
saw something different. One
a waterfall, one a lava flow, one a forest
primeval. Coming home, I took it off
and forgot it on the bus. When I told
my wife, she laughed and said,
Did you really think I'd give you a tie
made of the thread of life? That was a tie
made of silk, which is the memory
of cocoons, which are wombs, you were wearing
birth. I told her her thoughts
are the happy childhood I didn't have.
The sun was in her hair, where it stayed
until she combed it out that night.

Listen

She ran backward on a ship sailing forward
toward a man running west on a world
spinning east, waving at her
running out of ship waving at him
running out of her, until finally
they were so far apart, it was expedient
to write a novel in which a woman
tears pages from her notebook and drifts them
on the sea, which reads the story aloud
to the moon as it carries the words
to the wrong man, who dresses himself
in the novel and walks the countryside,
until one day, the right man
finds the wrong man dying
by the side of the road, and offers him
water, and reads the wrong man's chest
and arms and thighs, the word *sun*
in her handwriting casting a shadow
of the word *tree*

A country mapped with invisible ink

Like we are the hole that grows in poor, unmendable
nothing: we blind needles: we unmoored threads:
like feeling I'm the enaction of a waterfall by my tongue

upon your body, as when a boat is brought to the edge
of exile and a hand extends to a hand or a tree
beseeches with its shadeshawl: however born,

there is reaching, we agree the wind smelled of copper
one day, a passport the next: like how to escape
my brain's slum of words, the ghetto of the said,

while adoring there the rocks, the teacups,
if half of me is a Molotov cocktail and half
the inflection of loss and half a genuflection

to breath: like wondering if this extra half
is a country mapped with invisible ink:
like how windows ask to come along with the going

and preside over the staying, and I look at them
with all the love, all the shatter I can muster:
shards cutting me when I try to put the sky,

the distance back together: boredom cutting me
deeper when I don't: like searching for a man
in a burning house and finding a piano as echo flees:

a whetstone still warm from the blade: sheets pressed
with brainfolds of sleep: a whisper from the bathroom
of running water: but no body: and I carry

these things to safety that are not the man: the piano
in my arms, running water in my mouth, the vespers
of sleep, the knife, so like a wing, like flight:

and say of him, that was me, to the ashes, the char:
and sift the memory of flames for their sorrow,
holding smoke to the mirror interested only

in solid dreams: like it will finally see
what isn't there and give it my face, this presence
of absence I have tried and tried not to be

Elegy to unnamed sources

Attempts to say a thing:

Took a day off from breathing
to see if that would be like talking to you.

I've tasted your ashes twice, once today,
once tomorrow.

I study a dead tree that has a living shadow
made of God and crow shit, it resembles winter
all summer, what a stark easel the sky
never asked to be.

If you see a man chopping down wind,
it's me or someone who resembles me, with calluses
and an untied anchor falling through the ocean of his body.

A critique of the attempts to say a thing:

Grief is punch-drunk
stupid, that's why we get along, we have the same
empty IQ, the same silhouette of a scarecrow
challenging lightning to a duel.

A final attempt to say a thing:

It was the worst decision of my life, to hold
your last breath, to say anything out loud, anything
in quiet, I should have left it to the professional stabbers
in white, the professional pokers in squeaky shoes,

I had no business trying to see you leave, see death
arrive, I owe you an apology, an elegy, I owe you
the drift of memory, the praise of everything,
of saying it was the best decision of my life,
to hold you full, hold you empty, & live
as the only bond between the two

The missing

They go to the woods, the town, the entire town
looking for a girl but finding
a different girl with her own
missing eyes, her own beetle
in her mouth. They circle, the town,

the entire town, this wrong girl
whose splintered repose
appears to be running
against the side of the Earth,
who makes them imagine
this same becoming
for the right girl. We should lift her,

one is thinking, bury her
under the modesty of leaves, another,
and another
wants to burn the woods, shoot the crows,
poison the coyotes, and beneath
those thoughts, wants to touch
the wrong girl, reach
where she is open, into death,
as some would rest their heads
between the teeth of a lion. They turn,

the town, the entire town,
to where the priest
considers that the closest
he's come to a miracle
is when he backed out of a room,

the woman naked
on a bed, smiling, his pants
undone, his life
pointing where it had never been.
He sees them expecting him

to bring God into the moment
and wants to tell them, *God is here,*
God was here the whole time,
but instead, makes the sign of the cross
and asks them to pray silently
for the girl. Then it's dark

but no one leaves, then it's light
and they've grown accustomed
to the habits of ants, no one
wants to let the wrong girl go,
who is more of a scrap
every moment, as if they know
it's not their mourning
they tend but the mourning
of those from another town. Where

the right girl might be alive
in a kitchen, reminding the woman
who asks the right girl
if she knows her phone number,
of her own daughter's
pride of knowledge, her slow pleasure

in repeating seven digits, in holding
what is not real and making it
seem so, as flesh does,
until it does not.

Some recent weather

The rain is pregnant with a shape
exactly like you, late to tell your lover
it's over, who is late to tell you
he never loved you, also in the rain,
as wet as a goat in the rain or a statue
of rain in the rain, if there is one,
would have epaulets of rain in the rain
and be made of bronze or toffee, you are running
now in the rain, your version
of the human spirit, your very private instance
of converting sunlight when available
into vitamin D, for the energy
to believe we are more than energy, hoping
that you are wrong in the rain,
that it will never be over, as he
is hoping that he always loved you
in the rain, three blocks, two blocks, one block
to go and there he is, more lickable
than prophecy, like dew has taken human form
and put on a yellow shirt and shaved
in the rain, the rain so hard
you fuck in the rain and no one notices, the rain
fuck-shaped where you are fucking, an animal
with its mouth to your ear, and you
an animal with your mouth to its ear, everyone
on equal footing in the rain, the rain
speaking to your panting with its panting, the rain
washing away the rain

Born again

One day I was introduced to a bed
in which a woman was born, gave birth, and died.

The woman who introduced me to the bed
was the granddaughter of the woman
who was born in the bed and never lived
in another house.

Being a child of wind, I whispered
in the company of so much permanence.

The woman found my reverence ridiculous.

I knew this because she took off her clothes
and got on the bed as a way of asking me
to join her in making the bed a living bed.

It was in that bed that the woman told me
she tried to kill herself at seventeen.

Lots of Valium under a tree with horses nearby
ignoring her to eat.

This is my second life, she said, *the one I got
for not knowing more about drugs, for being shy
when it came to my father's shotgun
in my mouth.*

By then, she'd lived a hundred years
in dog years beyond when she'd wanted to die.

When I told her this, she said, *Woof.*

The bed squeaked each time we turned
or breathed our bodies into each other.

I keep asking myself if this story is true.

I seem to believe it is, seem to admire time
and making love on top of musical springs
and the world every day for not killing itself,
not exploding or burning down
as it might reasonably want to.

And the woman?

I seem to know her or contain her or think
the valley in which I live
would resemble her if someone had the language
to convince it to rise and be a woman
wearing a flowered dress.

Women are more likely to wear gardens
than men, to be valleys, to hold time
in their bodies and take us
inside what is passing
as it passes, what is arriving
as we leave.

And the man?

I seem to be him or want him
to be the feeling that stars
would look down on us and ask
What are you going through
if only they had mouths.

Scarecrow overhears himself thinking

I love crows, so midnight at noon. Me,
a suit stuck on sticks
that no longer suits your life. As if this aways
who you are, your self-imposed
supposes: suppose this is it — this field,
this light? What does, anyway, fill you
if not sun up or down, if not harvest,
yield? We should switch, I'll hop off
and gimp around, you'll hang
among scavengers for company,
for keeps, your straw-thoughts pecked
by wind. Are you me alive or am I you
dead? I lied: I hold my arms wide
not to shoo but greet, to say
to plunder, *Feel free, dig in.*

Elegy's

almost eulogy, is nearly dearly
beloved, I am un-gathered here
where you are not, I confess
I obsess, repeat myself to feel
this speaking's more than the creaking
of a pew in an empty church, where
as a tyke, surrounded by an absence
I was priestly asked to think of
as love, I couldn't wrap my mind
around such a zilch, whereas you
I touch and smell in the rough flesh
of memory, the word sonically
wants to be *remember me*, in my head
at least, you thrive some, you die some
daily in this weird-ass and misty mix
of ghost and gone, to which
I address what pretends to be
litany but is no more
evolved than this stuck
list: come back, come home

Desire

Having assumed it's none of my business
that our cats sniff each other's asses
while I prepare their breakfast, I turn now
to the window and resume the relationship
I've had with two horses who may be
two different horses since I fell in love
with shapes moving horse-like
in the distance eight years ago. I watched

one dusk in Michigan a horse mount
and conspire with another to make
yet a third, the mounted horse
completely not stopping eating
while the other quickly did his thing,
which resembled my thing in how it held on to
and cherished blood, as if for a while
it were a heart. I didn't expect that thought
but there it is, the dick-heart, and weirdly,

when I put their food down, the cats usually
go look at birds, as if to remind themselves
what the real life is
and that it isn't this one, though for me,
this has been completely authentic
from day one, such that if you gathered
all of my desires in a bag, I would marvel
at the size and hunger of the bag
and want that too, and we could talk
well into the night about how to slip the bag

holding everything into the bag
holding everything without dropping a thing,
like where else could you fit the sky
but the sky?

Take care

Nuclear missiles are rusting in their silo sleep,
gaskets are failing, firing mechanisms are going bad
but the engineers who designed them are retired
and records weren't kept, we couldn't make the missiles
today if we wanted to, and the thousands we have
might work if fired but might not, or leak, or go off
because they feel like it, *Why are we talking*
about anything else, I said to the waiter when he asked
if we had any questions. He cried and sat on one

of the two extra chairs at our table, one of the two spots
for emergency seating that were in our control,
then a second waiter came up and wondered aloud
if we were ready to order, I asked to hear
real silence, not the kind with my breath inside it,
my wife wanted the moon to make up its mind, to be full
or empty but nothing in between, our new friend
the first waiter wanted the second waiter
to make us take it all back, to tell him the missiles
were fine, that we knew how to repair death
on the magnificent scale of the atom. *That's the least*

we can do, I told the second waiter, *look at how*
we've wounded his face, it suggests a painting
by Francis Bacon that's been chewed on by a dog.
So we told our new friend the first waiter
that we were circus people, that we lie about everything —
there is no Strongest Man on Earth, The Lion Woman
has more ocelot in her than lion — he smiled, the world

had been healed, and he rose, and served his country
beautifully that night, bringing it sustenance
over and over on plates large enough to hold a human head.

Obituary for the middle class

This whole thing, this way of living beside a can opener
beside a microwave beside a son beside a daughter
beside a river going to college, you get up
and kiss the mortgage and go go go with coffee-veins
and burger-fries and pack your soul on ice
till sixty-five, when you sit down with a lake
and have a long talk with your breath
and cast your mind far away from shore, fish nibbling
the mosquitoes of your thoughts: they will whisper of this life
a hundred years from now to children before sleep
who will call them liars, "Once upon a time,
they had two and a half bathrooms and tiny houses
for their cars and doctors who listened
through tubes to their fat hearts, they named
their endeavors and beliefs *four-wheel drive,*
twenty-percent-off sale, summer vacation, colonoscopy,
variable-rate loan, inheritance," and we will be
as gods to them in that they won't believe in us,
and we will be spared the eternity of their worship
as they will be spared money, the counting
and the having and the memory of the middle share
of what gets harder and harder to call a pie

Song of the recital

for David

A man plays guitar beside the second-oldest river
is low in the world. That can change any minute. The Nile
is older than guitar, more Egyptian than the porch
is falling. A house from 1854, undulant floor, a train
goes by between the river is falling and guitar. A song
derived from the tango runs like a shudder through his hand
to the night is soft with the pliancy of bats. This one
javelins his voice at the stars have removed their veils.
This one lifts her anvil to the moon keeps to itself
but shines its diffidence upon the elms. A man
sets his guitar free on the river muttering homeless
to the north, fingerprints of music on the sandbar
I have been in various guises of my drowning.
Folding chairs applaud as grapes appreciate the chance
to live one hundred years as wine. A man plays a song
that is eternal as long as we're here to listen
we might as well paint the river with our faces. The tango
shudders like a hand up the dress of how hard it is
to be what experts call "yourself." If you set your breath
by the river, it's always time to shine to go.
People keep flicking the porch-light on like they miss
the sun is doing meth on the other side of the world
if you ask me to stay I'll stay receptive to the chance
we can strike the matches of each other's heads
without burning the minutes down. Don't take my word
for the juicy fragility of beauty: ask the baklava.

Leave a message

When the wind died, there was a moment of silence
for the wind. When the maple tree died, there was always a place
to find winter in its branches. When the roses died, I respected the privacy
of the vase. When the shoe factory died, I stopped listening
at the back door to the glossolalia of machines.
When the child died, the mother put a spoon in the blender.
When the child died, the father dug a hole in his thigh
and got in. When my dog died, I broke up with the woods.
When the fog lived, I went into the valley to be held
by water. The dead have no ears, no answering machines
that we know of, still we call.

Blue prints

Up and up, the mountain, but suddenly a flat spot
exactly the size of the house they would build,
and when they went to dig for the foundation, the foundation
appeared, just as the beams for the floor, as they started
to set them in place, revealed they had always been there,

it was like coming into the room to find your diary
writing itself, she told the interviewer, who wanted to talk
about her paintings but she kept coming back to the house,
including the sky above the house, how it resembled
her childhood, forgetting how to rain
when it wasn't raining, remembering blue
just when she needed to be startled most, don't you think

it odd that my life has always had just enough space
for my life, she asked the man's recorder
as much as the man, hoping the recorder
would consider the question and get back to her, then you moved
to Madrid, the interviewer was saying, and started painting
your invisible landscapes, I remember the first window

we lifted into place, she replied, that the view of the valley
it would hold was already in the glass when we cut the cardboard box
away, we just lined them up, the premonition
with the day, he had twenty more questions

but crossed them off, *I have always wanted to build a room
around a painting*, he said, *Yes*, she replied, *A painting
hanging in space*, he added, *A painting of a woman*

adjusting a wall to suit a painting, she said, *Like how the universe began,* he suggested, *Did it begin,* she wondered, *is that what this is?*

What the great apes refer to as a philosophy of life

Looking for someone to mug, asking politely
Can I mug you, a kindly grammarian responds, *May I mug you,*
and hands me her purse, her child, her mortgage,
I have to feed the child and pay for the house, a small thing
like the smell of piss in the streets
makes me nostalgic for New York in '82, when everyone
was mugging everyone, it was more
like a cultural exchange or a kind of greeting, I'm worried
about the child's standardized test scores,
about how I look carrying a purse, it's not my color
and styles are always changing, just last week
I was looking for someone to kill, the week
before that, someone to scold me
for not being an intravenous drug user, these things,
God does these things like send us halfway out
on a rope bridge before telling us
He's changed His mind about rope,
it shouldn't exist, it's not going to exist
any moment, like we are not going to exist
any moment, and I have never applauded a grape
in an alley, I have never put my hands around the face
of a stranger like a chalice, there's so much to do
if I want to be fully human, not three-quarters
or half or sort of human, I have to hoist you
on my shoulders so you can jump over the wall,
I have to build the wall higher, I have to catch you
on the other side, I have to shoot you
for trying to escape, I have to call your mother
and tell her you won't be coming home, I have to set

another place, I have to gather rain
into a body and make love with the rainbody
and teach the rainbody to moan and be taught
by the rainbody how to fall apart
into the most beautiful future reaching of grass
with its billion billion somnolent tongues
into the quiet applause of sunlight, into the pliant embrace
of air, may I mug you, may I kiss you,
may I sit with you on the veranda or build with you
such verandas as we need, such skies
as will hold the verandas in their arms, such martinis
as Plato never went on about or I'd read him
more often, sure the cave, sure the fire, sure the shadow,
sure we're stuck, but a drink now and then
makes philosophy more bearable, in that it's hard
to hold a drink in one hand and a book
in the other hand and a hand
in your other other hand, I choose the drink
and the hand hand over the drink
and the book hand, these are my priorities,
if they suit you, we can may share

The order of things

Then I stopped hearing from you. Then I thought
I was Beethoven's cochlear implant. Then I listened
to deafness. Then I tacked a whisper
to the bulletin board. Then I liked dandelions
best in their Afro stage. Then a breeze
held their soft beauty for ransom. Then no one
throws a Molotov cocktail better
than a Buddhist monk. Then the abstractions
built a tree fort. Then I stopped hearing from you.
Then I stared at my life with the back of my head.
Then an earthquake somewhere every day.
Then I felt as foolish as a flip-flop
alone on a beach. Then as a beach
alone with a sea. Then as a sea
repeating itself to the moon. Then I stopped hearing
from the moon. Then I waved. Then I threw myself
into the work of throwing myself
as far as I can. Then I picked myself up
and wondered how many of us
get around this way. Then I carried
the infinity. Then I buried the phone.
Then the ground rang. Then I answered the ground.
Then the dial tone of dirt. Then I sat on a boulder
not hearing from you. Then I did jumping jacks
not hearing from you. Then I felt up silence. Then silence
and I went all the way.

How we came to live where we live

The movie was over except the credits,
music like but not Satie, I don't remember
if I felt the loss of the child deeply
or needed people to think I did,
as when you stand before a painting
in a museum for as long as you hope
says something good about you, even
when you're not sure what that good thing is,
that you're considerate of red or appreciate
the historical significance of the brocade
or know that the woman in the foreground
holding the scythe was the painter's lover,
Mary Blake, who went on to swim
the English Channel twice, once forward,
once backward, but the vision was clear, I wanted
to carry tiny people around in a box, actors
who longed to perform *Our Town*
for an audience of any size, the numbers
didn't matter if their attention
was complete, *You would feel like the sun,*
wouldn't you, when they applaud, I longed
to ask the tiny actors in my arms,
and to feed them like the grasshoppers
I believed as a child only needed grass
in a jar to thrive, then we had cocooned
ourselves in our coats and were outside
with the gargoyles on the library, a gray sky,
I was carrying the box of actors
in how I believed the world was trying
to be perfect, nothing has to be real

to be real, like love, how often it makes me want
to eat you, not figuratively but actually
devour the hours you fill, one by one
or fill you, however that works with time,
and we walked until we couldn't, so far
there was no more light from the city,
and built a bed there, a garden,
a perspective, what you might call
the staples of a life, and stayed.

The heart of the soul of the gist of the matter

In college, I stole a human heart from the anatomy lab
and bowered it in a bird's nest that had fallen, I make
symbols, not whales, plagues, thistles, stars
are the moms and pops of everything
except themselves, *inanimate*'s the one word
I'd execute by guillotine to excise the lie
of lifeless, since bite into any bit of dirt
or dust and you've got a gob full of electrons
and quarks, the whole menagerie of matter's
in there, pinging and swooping, steel's got a pulse
as far as I'm concerned, and while I'm French
Revolutioning my way across the lexicon, I'll nix
miraculous too, for what isn't, what stone
doesn't do a number of things I can't
very well, avalanche and slingshot and skip
at the shore, where compared to my one, water speaks
with infinite mouths, and the simplest chair
is sometimes the most mystical being
in a room, animate with the knowledge
of how to be wood and supportive, alive
with the atomic breath of being, this is god,
small g, no Bible, Koran, I stole a human heart
from the anatomy lab in college and bowered it
in a bird's nest that had fallen, they looked
lost alone but thrived as partners, the dead heart
and dead home alive with the promise of shelter

To speak somewhat figuratively for S.

We went to the top of a building to jump off.
She could no longer deal with having been raped.
I was tired of falling asleep by looking forward
to never waking again. It was a perfect day
to watch a documentary on famous parachute-
folding mistakes. Then we had a final meal, final smoke,
final shower with the window open and pigeons watching.
Are you sure you wouldn't rather shoot the man
who did this, I asked, adding that guns are easier to buy
than "get well soon or whenever you want" cards. Of course
I knew her mother would never forgive her
if she shot her father, she'd have to shoot her mother too,
which would anger her sister, also raped, who'd wonder why
she didn't think of that herself. The only time
they talked about it, they were drunk on the steps
of our brownstone and throwing peanuts at cabs
until one cab backed up and a man got out
who was three feet tall but his arms were eight feet long
and it was the arms that did the talking. They ran.
A three-foot-tall man dragging eight-foot-long arms
is an interesting nightmare to watch run. They ran the whole night
together, all the way to Brooklyn and bloody feet
and crying most of the way out and laughing
most of the way back, I think what's known as a bond
was formed. Still she wanted to die and I wanted
to be with her, so we went up into the winds
people don't realize are in love with tall buildings
and debated a long time the virtues of taking turns
or going as one by holding hands and not shouting
Geronimo. I've often wondered why people shout that

when they jump and not *Ulysses* or *Grover Cleveland*,
I'm sure there's a reason like I'm sure her father
could explain himself if she held a knife to his dick.
We didn't jump — this is a poem — but she's still raped
and I still wish I could articulate the point
of breathing and her sister's still fun to have around
because she juggles really well and they lean
against each other in doorways without knowing
they're the only two trees of a very small forest,
in which I think of myself as a wild animal
sheltered deep within their shade.

Absence makes the heart. That's it:
absence makes the heart.

Here is where spiders set up shop
during the night, here is where a crow
decided to perch. Then it got up
and perched over there, beside
where another crow perched last week.
It would be peaceful to be a sail

except during the storm.
During the storm, I would like to be
the storm. If you're the storm,
there's nothing frightening
about the storm except when it stops,
then you're dead and the maps
are drowned. Within my heart

is another heart, within that heart,
a man at war writes home:
this is like digging a hole in the rain.

A very small bible

Jesus with amnesia walks
among the dead and wonders
why they don't rise, at least
one of them, as he seems
to recall someone did, and missing
their eyes, kneels and opens them
for hours, until his fingers hurt
and he's tired of the consistency
of how what isn't there
isn't there, like death
has no imagination, and hears
this name being called, *Jesus*,
from every direction and begins
calling too, to join
how this valley clearly wants
or needs to sound, that's
an interesting question, the difference
between need and want, he thinks
and thinks it will be dark soon
and where do I live
and is someone
waiting there with water
and to ask
with kisses, where have you been?

Notes for a time capsule

The twig in. I'll put the twig in that I carry in my pocket
and my pocket and my eye, my left eye. A cup
of the Ganges and the bacteria from shit
in the Ganges and the anyway ablutions of rainbow-
robed Hindus in the Ganges. The dawnline of the mountain
with contrail above like an accent in a language
too large for my mouth. A mirror
so whoever opens the past will see themselves
in the past and fall back from their face
speaking to them across centuries or hours
or the nearnevers it'll take mirrored someone
to unearth these scraps, these bones.
The word *terror*. I'll bury the word *terror*
to be free of the terror of the word *terror*.
I'll bury the word *terror* so it will scream
at mirrored someone as he or she falls back. Screams
how afraid we were that we were not afraid
enough. It's the morning of September 11th.
I'll be told all day how to feel about the morning
of September 11th. Told how to mourn the morning
of September 11th. If *terror* is said
seven times in a row, it loses meaning, becomes
humdrum, a mere timpani of ear.
If *terror* is said seven hundred
thousand million trillion times, I am being raped
by a word. I feel it was clever
to fly planes into buildings, that evil
is clever in the way rust is clever, eating itself
as it goes, that peace is clever in the way a stone
is clever, and I'll tuck a stone

from my garden inside a bell
wrapped in a poem about a bell, the poem
wrapped in the makings of a slingshot, the makings
wrapped in the afterbirth of a fox, the afterbirth
wrapped in the budget for the Defense Department.
So mirrored someone will face the question
of what weapons to make and what forgiveness
to perfect and what to honor in nature
and what to abhor in the nature
of what we do. These
are our complicated times
so far, my complicated time capsule
so far. My lament so far, my praise
so far as it takes me: to a hole
it takes me, to a shovel, to putting wind
in, the keen, the mean, but also
the hush, the blush, the dream
of getting along free of froth
and din. Clearly I need, I need, I need
a bigger box.

Another holiday has come and gone

It's shoot-an-arrow
into-your-ceiling day, I'm out of arrows,
I go to the neighbors
to borrow a cup of arrows, they're making love
on the floor doggy style, in that
she barks then he barks
at her barking, then it's over
and they circle in front of the door
to be let out, *We're trapped,*
I tell my lover later
on the phone, *Do you mean us,* she asks, I lie
and tell her *No, I mean every other person*
but us, we are free, we
are entirely wings and little bits
of fog and the open windows
of speeding cars and Carmen
at the end, when the performers
take their bows to the rush of air
from between our palms, forgetting
she is deaf, that she's heard nothing
I've said, that this is a poem,
that I am out of arrows and more
importantly out of bows

Ink

I feel obligated to get a tattoo.
It's how the skin of the species
is evolving. If I continue
living without plumage,
it will be impossible to mate
or hold a conversation
with a banker. My favorite
is strawberry ice cream. Not
average-size scoops, Baskin-
Robbins-size scoops
but three and tiny
I discovered one night
tattooed to a thigh.
It was the possibility
of kissing a private dessert
I so admired. I've decided
to get tattoos of my eyes
on the inside of my eyelids
so I can stare at the oceans
of my dreams. I'll have
muscles tattooed to my chest,
money to my palms, the smell
of honeysuckle to my breath. I want
BREAK GLASS IN CASE OF FIRE
tattooed to my brain, mouths
to the bottom of my feet, you
to me. There is not
enough art in this life.
Tattoo my front door
to my tombstone and place

a key on my tongue
like a mint. It's not for me
to decide whether my return
will be called
breaking out or breaking in.

Shed and dream

Rest with me under the linden tree.

I do not have a linden tree.

Come with me to buy a linden tree, stopping first
at the bank, for I need a loan to buy a linden tree.

Stay with me while the linden tree grows.

We can have babies while the linden tree grows,
colorectal cancer while the linden tree grows,
an infestation of ladybugs while the linden tree grows.

Babies sleep on blue blankets in July,
shadows of heart-shaped leaves
brushing their new faces as the linden tree grows.

Let us warn others of the hard work of the linden tree.

Then rest with me beside the knocked-down shed and dream
of the cherry tree.

O pie in the sky.

You can never step into the same not going home again twice

There was confusion on my end.
I thought Jesus was bringing the five-bean salad.
I thought the war had ended.
I thought I limped on the left side.
I thought the cloud a Lamborghini and got in.
I thought the zoo deserved a hacksaw.
I thought the tree had climbed the boy.
I thought the grenade a potato and ate it.
I thought Francis Bacon was painting my heart.
I thought bears would stop us
from killing the oceans.
I thought pole dancing had made a comeback.
I thought the Decency Party
would offer a full slate of candidates.
I thought the snow fort
a metaphor for the womb
of public housing.
I thought Zen Buddhism
would beat the New York football Giants.
I thought San Francisco
a roller coaster and screamed *whee*
into the ear of noon.
I thought you were alive
when I packed an extra pair of socks.
I thought you were alive
when I realized "manumit" was two down
on the plane.
I thought you were alive

when I asked a mutual bartender
how you were.
I thought you were alive
even when I peed Sam Adams a first time
after being told you were dead.
But I thought the war had ended.
I thought the half-moon was winking at me.
I thought cabernet on the roof
with two of your ex-wives a lovely funeral
ten years too late with jumping
at the end into the pool the only way
to prove I'd paid attention
to the jump shot with a second left
you'd always tried to be.
I thought a good, steady rain
would bring us to our senses.
But five thousand years
into the flood, I just don't know.

A poem that wanted to be a letter but didn't know how

Thank you Marianne Boruch

When, with the cadaver's skinned face
beside its open skull,
one of the other students
held up a stray left hemisphere
and spoke to this bit of brain
as to a phone, "She's not in
right now, can I take a message,"
I wanted there to be a story
our incursion had to tell
about the woman — that she "liked words — *Aesop's*
Fables, Housman. Frost by heart…
Not Jane Austen, she lied" — or to take
part of her home, nick spleen
or knuckle, and last night

reading your poem
in the almost-dark, with three deaths
on my mind, of who
who cares, the only difference
between my dead and yours
is everything, I got to this
and regretted I didn't —

"That *nothing* on and on, huge
and years, weighs
about nothing like
a whistle's sweet because
it's distant" —

and consider all the jars
I wasted, holding then and still
screws and jams
and more thorough nothings,
when of whomever she gray
and gutted was, there could still
be a smidge in the fridge, in my life, sick
but so are language and memory, which never
let the living let the dead die

Owe is to ode as whatever is to I don't know

I owe the crow, I know. Owe the watch,
the wrist, the swatch, the fist,
the sock, the crow, I know. Without clouds
I'd stand alone, without house
and switch and bomb and lock
and pick, there'd be no boom, no breaking in
to song for the crow, I know.
Owe every needle said *no*
to my arm, every leaf said *yes*
to the wind in my ear, owe wind
again, wind again
in this poem for the crow, I know.
When I'm dead, I want my head
to be an ashtray
in a bus station, tagged
at will by slugs and mugs
bound for Poughkeepsie and Kankakee,
my hips plunked into your garden
in lieu of my lips, after my kiss
is flown away by the hunger
of the crow, go crow. Owe maggots
for flies, flies for buzz, buzz
for saw, saw for seen, scene for action,
action for cut, cut for cure, cure
for sure, sure for shore, shore
for more, more for moon, moon
for flashlighting the night,
which falls softly
as the word *softly*
falls, and is wall-to-wall
crow, you know.

Ode to ongoing

People are having babies. Hoisting their children
to tree limbs on their backs and tying their shoes.
Telling them what the numerator is and why not
to eat one's boogers or not publicly
pee if at all possible to pee in private.
People are mixing their genes after wine
in romantic alleys and London hotels after crossing
a famous bridge. Trying to save for college
and not hit their children like they were hit
and not hit their children differently
than they were hit and failing and succeeding.
People are singing to wombs and playing the Goldberg
variations to fetuses who'll love Glenn Gould
without knowing who Glenn Gould is. I'm driving
along or painting a board or wondering
if we love animals because we can't talk with them
more intimately than we can't talk with God
and the whole time there's this background hum
of sex and devotion and fear, people telling
good-night stories or leaving their babies
in dumpsters but mostly working hard
to feed the future what it needs to grow strong
and prefer sweet over sour, consonance
to dissonance, to be the only creatures who notice
the stars or at least use them metaphorically
to go on and on about the longing we harbor
in such tiny spaces relative to the extent
of our dread that we're in this alone.

Elegy to the time it takes to realize the futility of elegies

Had I only dipped you in amber, only built an ark
and filled it with one of your kind, only been God
or a surgeon who was God or raised an army
of fire ants and bulldozers at the door
against what was coming, they say goldfish
forget immediately the circled bowl, they say elephants
come back to the bones of their dead and lift them
with their trunks, I did none of these things, forget
or lift your bones with my trunk, I like it here
in the fog, being touched by the cool washcloth
of the sky, had I only folded you into a triangle
like a flag that has thrashed all day
inside the monologue of the wind and needs to sleep,
never letting you touch the ground, coming to you
with my hand over my heart, pledging vibrancy
and odors and sunspots, I'm sorry for the snot
at the end, my face full of sheepshank knots
and nails, had I only been an ocean for you,
just a little one, a closet wide, a bedpan deep,
plenty of infinity for your fuse, your hovering,
the truth is I did all of these things, and let go
the steering wheel on the highway until the rumble strip
called me a dumbass, and chopped a tree down
and built a crib for a child, I like it here
when the fog erases itself and says, *I offer you*
the world freshly painted, including the woods
where you walked, if only I could weigh its shade,
would it be larger or smaller by exactly
the size of you, O science, give me such instruments
of knowledge, they are as passionately useless as poems.

Love

Lev and Svetlana are science students at Moscow University.
They fall in love. World War II happens. Lev goes to war and is captured
by the Germans. After the war, denounced by fellow Russians
who heard him speaking German, Lev is sentenced to death for treason,
his sentence commuted to ten years in the gulag. I am so far sorry
for Lev and Svetlana but not amazed. My amazement begins when Svetlana
breaks into the gulag, not once but several times, to see and touch Lev.
I have lived for three weeks as a man who knows this thing was done,
have washed dishes and dug a trench trying to imagine her first step
after closing the door, the first step Svetlana took under the power
of the thought, I am going to sneak into the gulag. I felt I knew the world
and then found out it contained that first step and every next step
toward guns and dogs and the Arctic Circle, it made me so happy
that she did this that I dug a better trench and washed cleaner plates
and tried to think of a place on my wife's body I'd never kissed.
I thought of such a place and kissed her there and explained
why kissing her there was the least I could do to show the world
I have a new and more generous understanding of life: I will get drunk
and throw knives at clouds but also kiss my wife's darkest privacy
to demonstrate I am willing to convert reverence to deed.
After I told my wife the story of Lev and Svetlana, she went to the ground
and put her hands around a dead plant and screamed at it to try harder,
she looked foolish and I loved her even more and joined her in screaming
at death, it made me feel Russian and obstinate and eternal, all good things
to feel, and where I kissed her isn't necessarily where you're thinking: maybe
miles into her ears and not with lips but words.

Elegy ode

Low clouds on the mountain about as high
as stars on top of a five-story building are
when I've gone up the fire escape
in my brain, where everything
is a mist and a slow wet kiss
meanders across the horizon
as the day's version of time, how I'll know
I haven't died has never been clear, it's raining
harder now than all the cups
I'll ever drink from could hold, a thirty-
by-thirty roof can fill a fifty-five-gallon rain barrel
after one-tenth of one inch of rain, I am a harvest
of such listenings to rivers and oceans
coming back to us from the sky, where they've gone
is where we see ourselves going, where everything
is a mist and a slow wet kiss
leads me back where I began, my father
leaning against my mother in a doorway, in a hurry, in a year
they'll be dead or ten, some soon
is the lit fuse trailing each of us, the clouds
like a wedding ring around the mountain
gone as of eight lines ago, I've been missing them
secretly before your eyes, as when we meet
and you say things or just stand there
helping your clothes not fall down, I've no clue
why mind-reading never caught on, I would page
after page of you and dog-ear and marginalia
is after all love, is tracks and we have come
as far in this moment as we might ever get, if this is the end,
I'm enjoying that crows haven't changed their story,

if this is the end, I have successfully
never worn cargo pants, if this is the end, I can admit
the orgy I've been trying to have
with everything leads naturally
to melancholia, for who has such long arms
as that, tongue as that, and to draw
one atom in is to let another go, I am afraid
I would try to name them all, how many Sallys
and Petes would that be, how many Keshons,
how many dust motes do I come across and feel
I'm being rude to by not adoring
more personally, more like the last chance
every chance is

Confessions of a nature lover

Back then I was going steady
with fog, who could dance
like no one's business, I threw her over
for a leaf that one day fluttered
first her shadow then her whole life
into my hand, that's a lot
of responsibility and a lot
of relatives, this leaf
and that leaf and all the other leaves
hung around, I told her
I needed space, which was true,
without it, I'd only be a soul
and no one's sure that wisp
is real, that's why we say
of real estate, *location, location,*
location, and of speech,
locution, locution, locution,
and of love, *yes, yes, yes,*
I am on my knees, will you have me,
world?

Circles in the sky

Dead things here
get a fan club
of vultures. It's cunning
to watch the sky admit
it wants to eat.

One vulture
tells another
tells another, theirs
is the largest wingspan
of sharing I have known.

What they'll do
to my once-dear
fence-leaping deer
is make it a dun sack
between road
and river engaging
in their voyages.

At least this hovering
of truly ugly birds
unless you look at them
metaphorically
reminds me to think
of someone I love
and prove it.

So if your phone rings
in a bit, it could be
sort of death calling

to ask, *How's it going,*
as I sort of hope
you'll be life answering,
Fine.

Something like an oath

It would be beautiful to wear a hat
of moonlight along the shops on a sunny day
when everyone has unpacked their faces
of work. Hopping on one stilt. Dragging the sea

behind me like a child with a puppy.
I have been a fence too long. I have kept a hive
for a head and kissed you with bees, and whispered
stings. It would be beautiful to hold a contest

for the eyes most like an opened jail cell.
I am tired of proving my heart a grenade.
It makes no sense when we are surrounded by fields
of genitals. It makes no peace to hammer

all day with my scowls against your temples.
I have been the calendar called Monday Monday Monday.
I have breathed like I'm swimming with an unrung
bell tied around my ankles. When I say my name

I hear a burned-down church. I have been
a dead crow shaving in the mirror. I have treated
the afterbirth better than my child.
It would be beautiful to go to the butcher's

and put the cow back together with vines
and semen and applause. No more axe handles
taking the place of ballerinas. No more apologizing
for the rudeness of bombs. Either we mean

to blow arms off or we don't. Either we have acid
in our veins or feathers or I am not a doctor.
I am afraid and swinging a pillowcase
full of doorknobs over my head to hold my place

on a rock a Roman stood on and thought,
I could conquer this, I could teach this wind
to bow. It would be beautiful to be the wind
saying, fat chance. To put the doorknobs back

on doors that once were trees we climbed
to be like our heroes, the birds and the sun
and the night was this huge kite I promised
myself I would one day hold the string of.

Elegy owed

In other languages
you are beautiful — mort, muerto — I wish
I spoke moon, I wish the bottom of the ocean
were sitting in that chair playing cards
and noticing how famous you are
on my cell phone — picture of your eyes
guarding your nose and the fire
you set by walking, picture of dawn
getting up early to enthrall your skin — what I hate
about stars is they're not those candles
that make a joke of cake, that you blow on
and they die and come back, and you,
you're not those candles either, how often I realize
I'm not breathing, to be like you
or just afraid to move at all, a lung
or finger, is it time already
for inventory, a mountain, I have three
of those, a bag of hair, box of ashes, if you
were a cigarette I'd be cancer, if you
were a leaf, you were a leaf, every leaf, as far
as this tree can say

Missing

I look forward to your tracks in snow
walking on their own down the mountain
while I think of you at the window
as someone who just hasn't called in a while,
having less and less an image of you
than a need to ask the fog
to come in and sit to tea, to solid motions
like integers hammering the world together.
You're not even pieces anymore,
not even bone scraps, and when I try to picture you,
my memory kills you all over again. A few
of the actual pictures I'd tattoo
to the parable of breath: the one that holds
the shadow of your hair against your cheek
for ransom, the one that stares at the back
of your head, the one of you on a cliff,
beyond which an island of bird shit
with seals warming their daily somnolence
reminds me of love and other misreadings
of nature, all of them versions of me
ironing the sky to wear to the séance
I keep wanting the wind
stuck on a barbed wire fence to be.
Imagination says things like that
without knowing what they mean. It means
there's all this wind and barbed wire
I don't know what to do with, that so far,
you've performed your tasks
as a dead person admirably, being no where

I've looked for you except barely in words
that just now dug up an apple tree
and moved it up the mountain, closer to rain.

As I was saying

Long, thin clouds like the sky is smoking.
I tell it to stop or share, it doesn't
stop or share, this is what happens
to my requests: they rise.
When I was a kid, a neighbor man
had a few and tied a cherry bomb
to a pigeon, it flew furiously
until kaboom. Feathers and bits
of what made the pigeon go
landed on the Smitky twins
playing hopscotch, they looked up,
I looked at them looking up, two of everything
the same, like their parents
knew the odds of needing a spare.
My wife wants to fly in a hot air balloon.
I say to her, *I'll wait here*
with the turtles. I try to save them
from getting squished when they cross the road.
They don't know it's a road or what a road
is for, getting away is what a road is for,
then coming back, then wondering why
you came back is what a road is for.
My wife's people are Ukranian, beets
are important to them. I tried to arm wrestle
her father once, he said, *Why*
would I do that: if I beat your arm
the rest of you will want revenge.
The other day, some kids
knocked a ball through our window,
one of them asked for it back, I said *Sure,*

if you give me the bat. He did,
then he asked for the bat, I said
If you give me the ball,
he started to hand it over
when I saw understanding
bloom in his face. That never happened
for me: understanding blooming in my face.
Not the way I wanted it to. So I'll die
and someone will have to deal
with what's left, the body, the shoes,
the socks. The last person on Earth
will just be dead: not buried or mourned
or missed. Like with kites, I cut the string
when they're way up,
because who'd want to come back?
So somewhere are all these kites,
like somewhere are all the picture frames
from the camps, and the bows
from hair, and the hair itself
I saw once in a museum, some of it,
in a room all its own, as if one day
the heads would come back and think,
That's where I put you, like I do
with keys when I find them in my hand.

Speaking American

When he learned I'm a poet he asked if I knew
this other poet. *We don't all know each other,*
I told him after he informed me she likes cheese
similes. Love is like cheese, time is like cheese,
cheese is surprisingly like cheese. Then I said,
I know this poet, and he went, *See.* "He went, *see*"
means he said see, see, but you know that
if you're American and alive. I explained
that "I know this poet" means "I know her work,"
when he was like, *Work?* "When he was like"
is like "he went," which is past tense of "he goes,"
in case you're from another country and confused
by our lack of roundabouts. *But poetry isn't work,*
he said, *unless you're talking about reading it.*
But I'm not talking about reading it, I went,
in a moment that was the future past of everything
I'd do from then on. Such as snag the last
of the hyacinth cookies and step onto the veranda
to be awed by stars. Where I went, *It's hard work,*
to be awed by stars: they're just little lights
about which we learn a song as children.
And he was like, *But I do wonder what they are,*
as both of us lifted our heads like birds
waiting for our mother to throw up in our mouths.
When I shared the image, he was like, *Gross,*
but then he went, *You're right, that's what we do,*
we expect the sky to feed us. This led
to a long discussion about yearning
in which the word "yearning" never appeared,
in which he went and I went and he was like

and I was like and the stars
kept doing what the song says they do,
because "burn your hydrogen burn your hydrogen
little star" doesn't fit the diatonic harmony
that pivots on an opposition between tonic and dominant
in a tune derived from "Ah! Vous Dirai-Je, Maman."
Then a woman came out wearing a red dress
the size of a whisper, lit a smoke
and the smoke's smoke acted all floaty
and sexy and better than us, and she was like,
Want one? and we were like, *Yes.*

Moving day

When it's time, the hotels of Ardmore no longer interesting
in their facades, the small bags of peanuts you used to buy
suddenly twice as big, as if someone far away, looking

out a window at a barge, had thought your appetite
was asking to be doubled, and the little girl you showed
how to affix playing cards to her spokes has gone off

to college, that school where anthrax arrived in a letter
and killed the chemistry professor whose face on TV
looked so small, like he'd been the head of a doll,

when you cried, fully and stupidly alone in your room,
literally into your hands, wiping the snot on your cat,
knowing this would set her about licking for hours, this spite

after emotion, you recognized it first when you were seventeen,
when you bit Sharon, not hard enough to break skin
but trust certainly was lost, and why, because she said

That must have been hard about military school, no longer
interesting because you've cataloged their moods, the different
shadows of the different cornices, the wrought-iron gate

so recently improved no longer sings when it opens, and you
should go, a whole new city, boxes of your life
staying closed, most of them, in stacks of who were you

after all, really, when it comes down to it, this collection
of how you said "shows to go you" to the magazine guy, of wearing
the apricot slippers, so have no set phrases, give your feet

a choice, I know, it's tiring, to be new, to even try, who am I
to judge, look at me, my head shaped just like yesterday,
and this appointment with language I keep, as if eventually

a handle will appear, and the sound of me saying *I'll turn it*
will be me turning it, to what, some sense of an other side,
which if you touch it first in your new home, in the away,

call me, the description, even with its holes, the torn edges
where to say a thing is to rip it, will be everything to me,
the beautiful frays.

Excerpts from mourning

Holding warm bear shit in my hand.

Thinking people like me
are weak who want to believe in angels
and people like me are stupid who refuse to believe
in angels.

Wanting to make love
to a rosary in a nun's hand.

Admiring the vertebra
of a cow on the table next to roses, roses beside keys,
four belonging to doors I don't recall
slamming or walking through or painting colors
of welcome, the music of absence
when I shake the keys, the absence of music
when I don't.

Heating a knife on the stove
and touching my forearm three times and living
with a scar resembling a cactus as the only painting
on my body.

Carrying ash of you to the Atlantic
(Kittery), bonebits to the Pacific (Point Lobos), giving you
to seals and otters and pollution, to waves and forgetting
and whales.

Wondering if I am inventing you
by remembering you or remembering you by writing of you
as silence sleeping inside a nest of shadow and hair.

Of breath
and shadow and hair.

Life

People in rooms drinking tea, drinking wine
in the same rooms and outdoors, taking trains
and driving and planting tomatoes
and harvesting tomatoes, kissing
or watching others kiss while wanting to be kissed,
a spider living by the stove
as tigers and grizzly bears roam Ohio
being killed after their owner
opened their cages and shot himself,
people talking about childhood
while holding babies, hands behind the heads
that can't support their own weight,
eating lunch and other meals at tables,
sitting at other tables smoking or wanting to smoke,
having a beer in a room before a funeral
and a beer in the same room after the funeral,
a spider living in the window as a woman
cuts all her hair off in Nome and mails it
to her mother's chemoed head in Memphis,
people going on too long and people
letting people go on too long,
standing in a doorway meeting the lover
of their son, taking her coat, her scarf, offering tea,
liking her smile, people drinking too much
and people letting people drink too much,
making beds for them, helping them in,
people sitting beside people under trees,
trees under clouds, clouds under sun, sun under
whatever sun is under and beyond reproach.

Sunny, infinite chance of rain

I don't want her to die.

She doesn't want her mother to die.

Five minutes after we were married, her father died.

The limo drove us to the hospital.

She stood in her veil at the side of his bed.

A nurse congratulated us.

We didn't know what words to put in our mouths
so we left our mouths empty.

I think of us as the top of a wedding cake
standing guard over the door his body had become.

She doesn't want me to die.

The Buddha said we shouldn't want anything but the Buddha
wanted us to believe that.

At the funeral, she wore a tricycle being pushed by her father
when she was five, her legs out to the side.

That's only true in this poem, like the cloud I'm looking at
is only true in this sky.

In all other skies, this cloud is a lie.

It's about to rain, not in the poem but in the thinking
that led to the poem,
the poem that helped me recall
I can still touch her entire body,
the soft parts, hard parts, bendy parts, all the places she'll hide
from everyone but me.

Everyone but the doctor and me, the doctor
and mortician and me.

In lieu of building a crib

for W

The day my child was born, I cut my hair off,
it came down to my waist, tied and twisted it
into a doll I gave her when she was strong enough
to hold a crow in each hand, *You looked*
like an ampersand when you were born, I told her,

we were under a tree, I'd been touching her toes
and saying *toe,* touching her head and saying
star, she clutched the hair-doll and did that thing
babies do, swallow us with the wells
of their eyes, I was never real until her stare

asked me to breathe all the way to the bottom
of my life, I'd been the cloud in the picture
of the baseball team, the brown scarf no one claimed
after the party, that seemed to float there
on its own, told her, *One day we'll burn that doll,*

it will brush the hour with smoke, it will mean hello
to a giant far away, she listened like a mirror, we have
the same expression of mind on our faces, the same
shadow of wondering in our eyes, told her, *This*
is air, it adores you, this is sky, it wants to be

a house, this is grass and grass is the color
of the promise I made with your mother, or maybe
I didn't say these things but thought
I'd been falling and someone pulled the ripcord
and here I am, a leaf on the ground

Equine aubade

Consider how smart
smart people say horses are.
I love waking
to a field of such intelligence, only pigs
more likely to go to MIT, only dew
harboring the thoughts of clouds
upon the grass and baptizing
the cuffs of my pants as I walk
among the odes. Long nose
of a thousand arrows
bound together in breath, each flank
a continent of speed, this one
quiet as a whisper
into a sock, this one
twitchy as a sleeper
dreaming the kite string
to her shadow has snapped. Old now
to my ways, they let me touch
their voltage, the bustling waves
of atoms conscripted to their form, this one
even allowing my ear to her side
so I can elope
with her heartbeat. I often feel
everything is applause, an apparition
of the surprise of existence,
that the substances of life
aren't copper and lithium, fire
and earth, but the gasp
and its equivalents, as when rain falls

on a hot road
and summer sighs. Or the poem
feels that, it's hard to tell
my mind from the poem's, the real
from the lauded horses, there's always
this dualism, this alienation
of word from word
or time from thrust
or window from greed. I am eager
to ride a horse out of the field, out of language,
out of the county
and to the sea, where whichever one of us
is the better swimmer
will take over, in case you see a horse
on the back of a man
from where you are
on your boat, looking at the horizon
in the late and dawdling company
of a small but faithful star.

I tell myself the future

The woods I got lost in as a child
When my father dies, naturally I'll want to call him
and tell him my father has died, he won't pick up, I'll decide
he's out raking leaves, that leaves are sullen, that I'm hungry,
that my father hasn't died, and when he finally answers,
I'll stand in the kitchen wondering why I called, most
of a peanut butter and jelly sandwich completed,
all that will remain is for the parts to be joined, the jelly
to the peanut butter wing, I'll tell my father
I'm cooking, he'll nod and I'll hear him nod

Good-bye

Small white church at the edge of my yard.

A bell will ring in a few hours.

People who believe in eternity will sing.

I'll hear an emotion resembling the sea from over a hill.

One time I sat with my back to the church to give their singing
to my spine, there's a brown llama you can watch
while you do this in a field if you'd like to try.

I don't think even calendars believe in eternity.

Beyond the church is a trail that leads to a bassinet in a tree.

Someone put it there when the oak and sky were young.

I'm afraid to climb the tree.

That I'll find bones inside.

That they'll be mine.

I want to be with my wife forever but not as we are.

She'll become a bear, I a season: Kodiak, spring.

Part of loving bagpipes haunting the gloaming is knowing
the bloodsinging will stop.

Beyond the church I pulled a hammer from the river.

What were you building, I asked its rust, *from water and without nails?*

This is where I get self-conscious about language,
words are love affairs or séances or harpoons, there isn't a sentence
that isn't a plea.

This is where I don't care that I'm half wrong when I say everything
is made entirely of light.

This is where my wife and I hold hands.

Over there is where our shadows do a better job.

About the Author

Bob Hicok's *This Clumsy Living* won the Rebekah Johnson Bobbitt National Prize for Poetry from the Library of Congress. Recipient of five Pushcart Prizes, a Guggenheim, and two NEA Fellowships, his poetry has been selected for inclusion in eight volumes of *The Best American Poetry,* including *The Best of The Best American Poetry.* This is his eighth book.

 Poetry is vital to language and living. Since 1972, Copper Canyon Press has published extraordinary poetry from around the world to engage the imaginations and intellects of readers, writers, booksellers, librarians, teachers, students, and donors.

WE ARE GRATEFUL FOR THE MAJOR SUPPORT PROVIDED BY:

THE PAUL G. ALLEN
FAMILY FOUNDATION

Lannan

THE MAURER FAMILY
FOUNDATION

NATIONAL
ENDOWMENT
FOR THE ARTS

WASHINGTON STATE
ARTS COMMISSION

Anonymous

Arcadia Fund

John Branch

Diana and Jay Broze

Beroz Ferrell & The Point, LLC

Mimi Gardner Gates

Gull Industries, Inc.
on behalf of William and Ruth True

Mark Hamilton and Suzie Rapp

Carolyn and Robert Hedin

Steven Myron Holl

Rhoady and Jeanne Marie Lee

Maureen Lee and Mark Busto

New Mexico Community Foundation

H. Stewart Parker

Penny and Jerry Peabody

Joseph C. Roberts

Cynthia Lovelace Sears and Frank Buxton

The Seattle Foundation

Charles and Barbara Wright

The dedicated interns and faithful
volunteers of Copper Canyon Press

To learn more about underwriting Copper Canyon Press titles,
please call 360-385-4925 ext. 103

The Chinese character for poetry is made up of two parts: "word" and "temple." It also serves as pressmark for Copper Canyon Press.

This book is set in two contemporary transitional typefaces. The text is set in Whitman, developed from Kent Lew's studies of W.A. Dwiggins's Caledonia. The heads are set in Mrs Eaves, designed by Zuzana Licko from her studies of Baskerville. Book design by VJBScribe. Printed on archival-quality paper at McNaughton & Gunn, Inc.